Bubby's Story

Contents

Forward

I met Bubby in January 1992, shortly after Dina (her oldest granddaughter) and I were engaged. Though barely five-foot-tall, her bright blue eyes, wide smile and vibrant energy made a powerful first impression. Her voice projected strength and confidence. Never have I heard English spoken so well in such a thick Polish accent. Bubby was poised and elegant, genuinely kind and unconditionally generous. Though always positive, I would sometimes sense in her a quiet sadness, nothing she would burden anyone with or let define her, but part of her all the same.

Whenever I spent time with her, she would tell me stories of her experiences in the Holocaust. Intrigued by the living history, I silently soaked up whatever she said. Often I would hear the same stories repeated, sometimes with more details or with a slightly different take. I would occasionally delicately try to slip in a question, however, it was usually a one-way dialogue.

In 1997, only after reading *The War Against The Jews 1933-1945* by Lucy Dawidowicz, a comprehensive and detailed history of the Holocaust, which describes conditions and events in the Lodz Ghetto and the suffering of the Jews confined there, did I start to appreciate what Bubby endured. I also arrived at the disquieting revelation that there are stories she must not be sharing.

My interest in the Holocaust then centered on Bubby's experiences, particularly in the Lodz Ghetto, and I began to read

1

several essays and books on the subject. One collection of writings, Joseph Zelkowicz's chronicles of daily life in the ghetto *In Those Terrible Days*, affected me profoundly. His sardonic and rhetorical style of prose caused me to empathize with what it must have been like and made me understand how the stories in Bubby's select repertoire were only what she was willing and/or able to reveal.

In May of 2017, I traveled to the Yale University Library in New Haven Connecticut to watch Bubby's interview in the Fortunoff Video Archive for Holocaust Testimonies, recorded 20 years earlier. Since then, her video testimony has been made available for viewing at various institutions and libraries around the world and I recently watched it again at the Cooke Library here at Towson University in Maryland.

In it I heard some stories for the first time, more details on stories I had heard before, and saw the effort she made to convey as best she could what she endured. After viewing her testimony, I felt a powerful obligation to share her story and to codify her experiences for our family; my brothers and sisters-in-law, her grandchildren, and our children, her great grandchildren, for posterity. As I began to write, I realized this story had to be more than just a collection of Bubby's firsthand accounts, it should include the historical details surrounding them. Weaving Bubby's story through the history of the Holocaust offers an opportunity to learn about it in a meaningful way; through the prism of her experiences.

The tentacles of the Holocaust touched wherever the Nazis held power or influence and consequently affected much of European Jewry and even Jews in parts of North Africa and Asia. Since this story is about Bubby, most of the historical details discussed in the chapters are limited to her circumstances in Poland and Germany. *Bubby's Story* though, is the story of the Holocaust as she lived through nearly every horrific stage of the "Final Solution" and the atrocities that defined it.

I often wondered about the motivation behind the Holocaust and how a civil society like Germany could have perpetrated it. In the summer of 2018, while paying a visit to Bubby, her daughter, Aunt Miriam lent me a book titled *Holocaust: The Nazi Persecution and Murder of the Jews* by Perer Longerich. This book was extremely informative and throughout *Bubby's Story,* in its Introduction and Conclusion, I attempt to convey what I learned from it and other research, in the hope that readers leave with a broad understanding of the Holocaust and find answers to many of their questions, as I did.

We should feel obligated as Jews and particularly those of us blessed to be part of the Schultz family, to learn about the Holocaust, understand how and why it happened, and be vigilant to reject any form of racism which could lead to another. Per the famous quote attributed to the Spanish Philosopher George Santayana, "Those who cannot remember the past are condemned to repeat it."

In honor of Bubby, let us never forget.

Respectfully,

David J. Dresin
Baltimore, MD

April 15, 2020

75th anniversary of the liberation
of Bergen-Belsen

Introduction

The Holocaust did not happen in a vacuum. It did not begin with a virulent, antisemite named Adolf Hitler, who led his National Socialist German Workers' Party (Nazis) to rule Germany. The seeds for the Holocaust were planted in Germany and the rest of Europe many centuries before.

The early Catholic Church of the medieval period was all-powerful and saw the Jews as a threat to their dogma. Consequently, Jews were isolated, ostracized, and persecuted. They became a convenient scapegoat and were accused of Blood Libels (baking Matzah with the blood of Christian children), purposely spreading disease, and causing dissent. This sometimes led to acts of violence against whole Jewish communities. The Jews, with no means to defend themselves and no government protections, suffered immensely during this period.

As Europe became more enlightened and the Church lost some of its influence, Jews were granted more freedoms and access to society, though deep-rooted antisemitism remained. Discrimination became less about religion. Jews were now being considered a different race. Scientific racism, the pseudo-science which claims there are superior and inferior races, became popular in the 19th century and was widely accepted in academic circles. In 1879, Intellectual anti-Semites such as the German Wilhelm Marr, posited in his book *The Way to Victory of Germanism over Judaism* that the Jews and Germans were engaged in an epic struggle that could only be resolved by the ultimate victory of one and total annihilation of the other. Édouard Drumont, a French journalist penned a popular book *La France Juive* (Jewish France) in 1886, which developed three strands of antisemitism: racial, financial, and religious. In 1903, a forgery of minutes taken at a supposed secret society of ultra-wealthy and powerful Jews aimed at global domination called, *The Protocols of the Elders of Zion* was fabricated in Tsarist Russia and widely disseminated.

Even in the United States of America, Henry Ford's newspaper *The Dearborn Independent* devoted 91 issues to what he considered the "Jewish Menace." These editorials were compiled into a collection of four volumes, 20 chapters each, published from 1920 to 1922 titled *The International Jew: The World's Foremost Problem* which happened to come out during the formative years of the Nazi Party. Hitler voraciously read much of the above and more. These widely circulated publications reveal how antisemitism was a part of mainstream Western culture at that time. This helps explain the lack of vocal outrage, quiet acquiescence, and even outright support by many Germans and other Europeans to the Nazi persecution of Jews.

In the beginning of the 20th century, the German hierarchy felt they deserved to be the dominant power on the continent. Being located in Central Europe however, made them vulnerable to France in the west and Russia in the east. Seeing Russia as their primary threat, they were eager to neutralize the massive country before it had a chance to modernize its military. Therefore, through their proxy Austria-Hungry, Germany instigated World War I.

World War I, lasting from the summer of 1914 to the fall of 1918, was an extremely bloody and costly conflict on all sides. The war of attrition and blockade wore down the German people and caused civil unrest. The Kaiser and German princes were forced to abdicate, and the newly elected Weimar Republic sued for peace. The subsequent Treaty of Versailles, was crippling and humiliating, requiring Germany to demilitarize, make territorial concessions, pay massive reparations, and take full blame for the war.

Many Germans, especially those in the military, believed they could have won by holding out a little longer and felt, "stabbed in the back." They blamed this betrayal on the communists, industrialists and the Jews. The new Nazi Party pledged to redress the hated Treaty of Versailles and used it to reinforce their antisemitic platform.

Mein Kampf, Hitler's ranting, vitriolic, racist, and antisemitic manifesto cloaked in lofty nationalist and socialist aspirations, discusses how the primary duty of the German State is to insure and promote the purity of the superior Aryan race. This was to be achieved through eugenics, one of the Nazi embraced pseudo-sciences that populations can be improved by breeding those with desirable, heritable characteristics (positive eugenics) and by segregating and sterilizing those with genetic defects or undesirable traits (negative eugenics). The one race in particular needing to be entirely uprooted from Germany was the nefarious Jew.

During the roaring '20s, much of the world experienced explosive economic growth, including Germany. In this time of prosperity, the fledging Nazi Party barely received 3% of the vote. That all changed after the U.S. Stock Market crash in 1929, dragging Germany into the "Great Depression." In an environment of massive unemployment and political strife, when Parliamentary Elections were held in 1930 and again in 1932, many Germans voted for radical change. The Nazi Party secured over 37% of the vote and was awarded 230 out of 608 seats. It was not long before Chancellor Hitler, through the Reichstag Fire Decree and Enabling Act, maneuvered to eliminate all political opposition and legally gain complete dictatorial control over Germany.

To the Nazis, antisemitism was much more than just racist ideology, it served a very practical, politically expedient purpose and formed the basis of what is known in German as "Judenpolotik." This "Jewish Policy" was adroitly wielded as a form of Realpolitik and used as a means to surreptitiously consolidate absolute power. The sanctioned terror unleashed upon the German Jews by gangs of Nazi SA (Brown Shirts) from 1933 onward and passively accepted by most of the German population, emboldened the Nazi controlled government to enact legislation excluding German Jews from society and the Nuremberg Laws of 1935, totally stripping them of citizenship. The vast majority of Germans unaffected by this, as Jews represented less than 1% of the population, may not have appreciated how the criminalization of race, enabling the Gestapo to insert themselves into all aspects of private life, granted the fascist Nazi State limitless power.

Economic laws were soon passed, culminating with actions taken after the Kristallnacht Pogrom in November of 1938, expropriating most of the German Jews' wealth. Hermann Goering, Hitler's second-in-command and Plenipotentiary responsible for re-arming Germany, took the billions of dollars confiscated from the German and Austrian Jews (Austria was annexed by Germany the previous March; Anschluss), to fund the re-armament effort.

Hitler's territorial expansion aspirations for the greater German Reich were not limited to Austria. In September of 1938, he coerced the cessation of the Sudetenland, the area around Western Czechoslovakia bordering Germany, and that March, occupied the remainder of the country. The Czechoslovakian Jews, just like the Jews of Austria the previous year, were now ensnared in the Nazi web and subject to all their racist laws and persecution.

Hitler was just getting started, and the only way to fulfill his dream of a thousand year Reich was through war. Another major tenet of Nazi ideology clearly espoused in *Mein Kampf* (had the British Prime Minister Neville Chamberlain bothered to read it like Churchill did, he may have had a policy for dealing with Hitler other than appeasement) was Lebensraum "Living Space." This Lebensraum policy was the Nazi impetus for Generalplan Ost (Master Plan for the East), the plan to settle Germans in Eastern

Europe through conquest and removal of the "racially inferior" populations there.

The ensuing war about to be unleashed on the continent would result in the death of nearly 60 million people.

1

Childhood

Janina "Yanka" Pinkus (Bubby) was born in Lodz, Poland on September 6, 1924. The second largest city in Poland behind Warsaw, Lodz was home to over 230,000 Jews, a third of the city's population. Lodz was a vibrant, modern city considered the "Polish Manchester", for its large textile manufacturing industry. Bubby remembers how shortly before the war, the city installed its first traffic lights.

Though an only child, Bubby had a large family. She had many first cousins her age, as her mother Miriem had five sisters and they all lived happily together in Lodz. Bubby's father, Abram Pinkus, had a successful judiciary notary practice, owned property and was well respected in the community. They lived in a comfortable flat at Srodmieska 72 (now Wieckowskiego), near the bustling city center.

Raised in an affluent, secular household, Bubby wanted for nothing and was afforded the best grooming and education. She was fluent in German, Polish and familiar with French and English. She did not however, speak any Yiddish, the ethnic language of the Ashkenazi Jews of Europe. This, more than anything, shows how cosmopolitan her family was. She would later learn Yiddish as a teenager, standing for hours in the bread lines.

Following the Nazi's rise to power in neighboring Germany, there was a noticeable increase of antisemitism in Lodz. Bubby's parents took her out of the more prestigious secular school she was attending with many non-Jews, to an all-Jewish school, which they felt would be safer for her.

Bubby was a good student, had many friends and enjoyed going to the movies. The 1935 film "Dante's Inferno" made a lasting impression on her. She could not have imagined then how much she would relate to it.

2
War

On September 1, 1939, Nazi Germany invaded Poland, triggering World War II. Five days later, ("My 15th birthday present," Bubby would say sarcastically) the German Army was on the outskirts of Lodz. As remnants of the Polish Army hastily retreated from the city's overrun defenses, tens of thousands of Jews fled east to avoid being under Nazi rule. On September 8, 1939, the Germans victoriously marched into the center of Lodz. Her father at that time chose to stay. He probably calculated there was nowhere to go that would be any safer. He was right.

The cruelty against the Jews began immediately. On Rosh Hashanah that year, all Jewish owned stores were forced to stay open and the synagogues closed. Soon, Jewish men were grabbed off the streets and forced to do backbreaking and humiliating labor.

They were dispossessed of their property and forbidden to conduct business. Certain educated and influential Jews were arrested, tortured, and then executed or sent to concentration camps. All Jews were forced to wear yellow Star of David patches sewn onto the front and back of their coats. Anyone caught not wearing one was arrested.

Some of the Poles and many ethnic Germans in Lodz willingly collaborated with the German invaders. Bubby remembers Polish children leading soldiers around town pointing out Jewish homes, which the Germans would subsequently loot. In Bubby's building, there lived a German woman on the top floor. Those small apartments were typically for domestic servants or other working-class people. Bubby had little interaction with this woman and did not even know her name.

Early one morning, shortly after the occupation, there was a loud knock on Bubby's door. It was the German woman from upstairs. Frantically, she told Bubby's father that soldiers were rounding up all the Jewish men in the neighborhood and that he should quickly come up to her apartment and hide. No sooner had she gathered up all the Jewish men in her building, then the soldiers arrived. As floor by floor they searched the building, thirty or so Jewish men huddled together in her small apartment in absolute silence. When the sound of the soldiers clicking boot steps reached the top of her stairs, she confidently strode out to meet them in the hallway. With a hearty "Heil Hitler" and salute, she proudly proclaimed in perfect, unaccented German that there were "No Jews living up here." Satisfied, the soldiers left.

Had they just peeked in her apartment, her and all the men would no doubt have been executed, or sent to concentration camps. Bubby did not realize it at the time, but this woman also saved her life that day, as Bubby never could have survived what was to come without her father.

3

Refugees

By November 1939, living conditions in occupied Lodz had deteriorated. The Germans controlled everything. Food was rationed and in limited supply. A friend of Bubby's father, a non-Jewish Pole, warned him that the Germans were planning to arrest all the remaining affluent Jewish men in Lodz. It was no longer safe to stay. Having heard things were better in Warsaw, they decided to go there as a family. Packing only what they could carry, they headed to the train station.

That October, Lodz was annexed by Germany into the Greater Reich. The part of Poland which contained Warsaw had not yet been annexed and was called the General Government, it was like another country. Travel documents were needed to get there and it was difficult for Jews to obtain them. Unable to go directly to Warsaw, Bubby and her family first went south to a city called Katowice. The situation there was worse than Lodz. They stayed just a few days until Bubby's father was able to bribe for the necessary papers. He did not want to remain in the Reich though he could not have imagined at that time how bad things would get for the Jews in Nazi controlled Europe, no matter where they were.

Upon arriving in Warsaw, they lived with another family, renting a room in their apartment. When winter came, it got very cold and food became scarce. Bubby's father went back to Lodz to check conditions and quickly sent word through friends that Bubby

17

and her mother should come home and join him as the food situation had improved some. Even then, Bubby noticed the first and foremost consideration on any and all decisions was food.

Bubby and her mother had to be smuggled back into the Reich; staying off the roads and traveling at night by horse driven sleigh. It was terribly cold and the ground was covered in a thick blanket of snow. At the border near Lodz was a German check point and people were not being allowed past. It was New Year's Eve and close to midnight. Suddenly, all the soldiers were gone. As luck had it, they left their posts to drink and celebrate in the warmth of their bunks. As 1939 became 1940, Bubby and her mother returned home.

They found their apartment ransacked. Their Polish maid had invited the Germans in to take whatever they pleased. Holes were punched in the walls, as the Germans believed Jews hid valuables in them. Her father did in fact hide money, which they did not find. He was a smart man and hid it in magazines. Even if they had been leafed through, the bills would not have been noticed between the pages, tucked in close to the spines. This money was very much needed for what would come next. As their apartment was now unlivable, Bubby and her parents moved in with her grandmother.

4

Ghetto

On February 8, 1940 it was announced that the Jews of Lodz were to be segregated to Baluty. Baluty was a slum neighborhood in the northern section of the city. Most of it did not have running water or a sewage system. Being well-connected, Bubby's father learned ahead of time the exact boundaries of the ghetto and rented an apartment in a nicer part of it, closer to the city center. This foresight enabled them to survive the ghetto together until nearly the end.

Lodz Ghetto

With nowhere else to go, some of Bubby's relatives moved in with them. Their small apartment now had 15 people living in it. Over 160,000 Jews were forced into an area less than two and half square miles. On April 30, 1940, the ghetto was sealed. No one was allowed in or out. Barbed wire fences and sentry boxes were placed

19

around the ghetto and anyone who got too close was shot. Food delivery to the ghetto was controlled by the Germans and distributed by the Judenrat (the ghetto's Jewish governing body), led by the German appointed Chaim Rumkowski.

According to historical records, Bubby's address in the ghetto was first Hamburger Strasse 40, Flat 8 (Lutomierska before and now after the war) and then Basar Gasse 10, Flat 20 (Bazarowa before and now after the war).

After the conquest and subsequent annexing of Lodz to the Reich, all the Polish street names were changed to German and the entire city renamed Litzmannstadt in honor of Karl Litzmann, a decorated World War I general from the Battle of Lodz in 1914, and a renowned Nazi Party member who died in 1936.

Bubby's addresses in the ghetto were across from one another and in the Southwest section, close to the fence. These buildings faced a park where they would sometimes hold executions which the ghetto inhabitants were forced to witness.

"He probably committed a terrible crime," Bubby would say sarcastically, "like stealing a potato." The cruel Nazis would not allow the bodies to be quickly buried per Jewish tradition and made them hang for days to send a message. Bubby had to pass by them and the murder of crows pecking their decaying flesh each day on her way to and from home.

Corralling the Jews of Western Poland into nearly 100 ghettos was to be, at first, a temporary measure to facilitate their organized transfer to a "reservation" in the area around Nisko and Lublin, Poland. After Germany conquered France in the spring of 1940, the resettlement of European Jewry to the island of Madagascar, a French Colony, "The Madagascar Plan" took on sincere consideration. Only after Winston Churchill's refusal to capitulate during the Battle of Britain and the indefinite postponement of Operation Sea Lion, the planned invasion of England, was the idea abandoned. With the mighty British Navy still in the war, the Germans would have no means of transporting millions of Jews to a faraway island in the Indian Ocean.

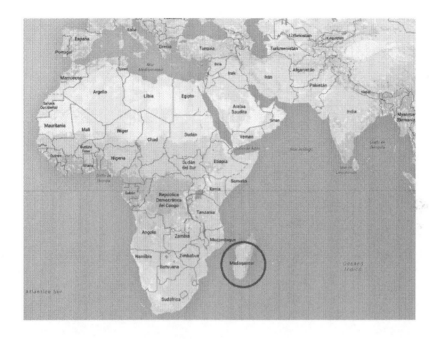

The next resettlement location for the Jews would be determined after the anticipated defeat of the Soviet Union following "Operation Barbarossa", code name of the invasion secretly being planned for the spring of 1941. The Nazis would then herd millions of Jews followed by tens of millions of indigenous "Slavic" people east into Siberia where most would likely starve to death or succumb to the harsh environment, clearing up huge swaths of Lebensraum for ethnic Germans and Germanized Aryans.

In the ghettos, the Jews were expected to cover the costs of their food and incarceration through work. In Lodz, over 100 factories were set up producing all sorts of products for the German military and commercial market. No wages were paid, only coupons for meager amounts of food. Money had no value in the Ghetto. People traded in their cash, jewelry, gold, and furs for "Rumkies", the slang term used for the ghetto currency established by Rumkowski. This "currency" gave the Judenrat and their German overloads complete control over the ghetto economy and dissuaded smuggling from outside. Everything was in short supply, especially food and severe hunger was pervasive.

In the beginning of the Ghetto, people tried their best to live as normal a life possible. Schools and a post office were established, lectures were held and musicians organized concerts and plays. One show Bubby remembers in particular had a child actor who loved performing, since there was a scene in which he got to eat a roll of bread. This entertainment offered much needed distraction to the misery of the ghetto. At least for a few moments, they could forget where they were, and feel normal.

Bubby made an effort to attend school every day. She always wanted an education and dreamed of one day going to college. School was freezing. They sat there shivering in their coats and gloves. Teachers sacrificed with no teaching material and students had to share one or two books passed around class. Bubby was always a good student but now under these circumstances, she and her classmates appreciated and thirsted for education more than ever and learned like they never had before.

The ghetto was filthy. Garbage was everywhere. Bubby could not wait to get home after school so she would not have to use an outhouse. Human waste was collected in tanks and hauled away to the outskirts of the ghetto by the Scheiss Kommando. They wound up covered in filth from this work but volunteered none the less for rations. Horses weren't used to pull these carts, the few horses allowed in the ghetto were considered more valuable than Jews and their meat a rare delicacy.

The ghetto was like a prison and had an 8pm curfew. Nights in summer were unbearably hot and freezing in winter. People broke apart their furniture and anything else they could burn for heat. As conditions worsened, people became more despondent. Malnutrition, overcrowding, and unsanitary conditions led to the spread of disease. On top of all this, their German tormentors were relentlessly on their backs. If they heard a rumor someone was hiding gold or jewelry they would be dragged into Kripo Headquarters and tortured. After two or three days, if they made it out alive, they were unrecognizable.

People lived in constant fear. They were powerless. There was no justice. Those of high caliber before the war turned into animals in the ghetto, doing anything for food. The Nazis could validate their assertions, through the conditions they created, that Jews were subhuman. One could wonder what the Germans would have descended to had they suffered such depravations and indignities.

In spite of all this, many still hoped the war would end soon and things would return to normal. No one could have imagined this nightmare would last for five more years.

5

Bridges

To not disrupt the flow of traffic in the city, two main thoroughfares, Zgierska and Limanowskiego streets (changed by the Germans to Hohenstiener Strasse and Alexanderhofstrasse respectively), were left un-diverted and cut straight through the ghetto. These streets were lined with barbed wire fences splitting the ghetto into three enclosed sections. Jews crossing these streets to get to other parts of the ghetto through guarded gates caused frequent traffic jams.

To resolve this problem, the Germans had three wooden pedestrian bridges built, two over Zgierska and one over Limanowskiego. For sport, the Germans soldiers patrolling below would sometimes indiscriminately shoot at the bridges. Bubby had to cross one of these bridges twice a day to get to and from school.

One day, Chaim Rumkowski paid a surprise visit. He arrived late in the day, keeping the students after dark. Bubby's mother nearly had a heart attack when Bubby did not come home on time, terrified what might have happened to her crossing the bridge. This illustrates the insensitivity of Chaim Rumkowski, who the Jews of Lodz mockingly referred to as "King Chaim" for his autocracy and hubris. He believed that ruling the starving ghetto with an iron fist would ensure his and some of the ghetto's survival and he would go down in history as a savior of the Jewish people. This was not only delusional but foolish. The Germans viewed him no differently than any other Jew with whom he would ultimately share the same fate. Bubby thought he was crazy and avoided all contact with him.

Soon, most of the schools closed and those that were able to remain open were part-time. Bubby got a job after school as the only way to get food was through work. She now had to cross two of those bridges, twice a day.

6
Work

With his connections and experience as a property owner and landlord, Bubby's father was able to get a job working for the Ghetto Housing Authority and later one for Bubby working at a women's girdle factory. Since he was friends with the factory's manager, Bubby was assigned to the office rather than being placed on the floor and was trained in bookkeeping. It was here, ironically, she learned the profession that helped support her and her family later in life.

As part of the executive staff and daughter of the manager's friend, Bubby sometimes received extra food coupons which she shared with her family. They were "fortunate." Families with more mouths to feed and with members too young and/or too old to work would starve.

Bubby contracted hepatitis but still dragged herself to work. One of her cousins suggested she check into the hospital. There she could at least get some sugar which was supposed to alleviate some symptoms of the disease. Bubby would not set foot in the hospital, no matter how sick she was. She heard horror stories of how the Germans would show up and randomly clear out patients and kill infants by slamming them against the walls, the blood stains still visible.

While at work, her boss was kind enough to let her rest her head on her desk. Had she been a laborer working on the floor, she would not have been able to do that. She would not have been able to stay at work and get her "Rumkies", she and her family likely would have starved to death.

7

Starvation

The food the Germans allowed into the ghetto was purposely not enough for everyone to survive. People ate rotting cabbage, potato peels, ersatz coffee made from ground acorns, whatever they could. Children too young to work and who had no school to attend would spend their days digging in heaps of garbage for scraps of anything edible and bits of coal to heat their homes or sell for food. They became the "breadwinners" of many families. No longer were there children in the ghetto, just little Jews.

Families were torn apart as they would often hide and even steal food from each other. One would place a piece of bread under their pillow when they went to sleep, only to find it missing when they awoke. Infants and toddlers were crying constantly; not understanding why they couldn't eat. People began to die from starvation. It was horrible. One day they would be all swollen and the next day dead. Most of Bubby's aunts, uncles and cousins died from hunger in the ghetto. After visiting relatives who were sick, Bubby's mother commented on how awful her sister looked but that Uncle Marcus, "really looks dead to me." Turns out her brother-in-law was dead and was lying in bed for two days before anyone realized it. No one thought it strange that he didn't get up. It was normal for people to just lie in bed and sleep us much as possible. There was no food, it was cold, why get up? That was how many people coped, how they escaped.

The overwhelming hunger blocked out rational thought and feelings. One of Bubby's cousins contracted tuberculosis at the age of 18, suffered for a year and died. Bubby never forgot when they got home from the funeral, the first thing her aunt asked after just burying her 19 year-old daughter was, "Is there any food here?"

All anyone thought and dreamt about was food. They would talk about their favorite foods before the war and what they going to eat after the war. When Bubby would discuss the Holocaust, the only aspect of the suffering she ever felt compelled to try and convey was the hunger. "There is no greater pain," she would say, "than hunger. Unless one experiences it, they can never understand it." Bubby lived with it for over 5 years. "It was torture." She said. "They tortured us. What more torture could there be" she added, "than for a mother to see her child go hungry?"

8

Deportations

At dawn on June 22nd, 1941, the single largest military campaign in history, Operation Barbarossa was launched. Nearly 4 million German and Axis soldiers simultaneously attacked the Soviet Union along a 2,000-mile front. The Nazi's war of ethnic cleansing had begun.

Over the next few months, hundreds of thousands of Jews in the newly occupied Soviet territories would be systematically murdered by the Einsatzgruppen (execution squads comprised of SS paramilitary and police units) and their collaborators. At first, their orders were to round up and execute communist leaders, Jews in government posts and loosely defined "radical elements", anyone who might pose a threat in any way to the occupation. Soon, all Jewish men between the ages of 15 and 45 were to be considered "partisans" and shot. To do some of their dirty work, the Einsatzgruppen would instigate and encourage Pogroms (mob violence against Jews), often with willing and gleeful participation, particularly in the Baltic States and Western Ukraine.

By August, the blood thirst of the Einsatzgruppen would no longer be satisfied with just men. Jewish women, children and the elderly were now targeted. The depraved rationale the Nazis used to justify the killing of children was: when Jewish boys grow up, they will seek revenge for the murder of their fathers, so should be eliminated now before they are a threat. As mothers would not willingly allow their little boys to be taken, they were just executed with them. Once age and gender were no longer discriminating factors, all Jews were now being murdered en masse with ever more orchestration.

From September 29th to September 30th, 1941, nearly 34,000 Jews from Kiev, Ukraine, mostly women, children and the elderly, (by then most military aged men had been conscripted into the Red Army) were ordered to gather for "relocation" in "retaliation" for rear operation bombing attacks by the Soviet NKVD against the recent German occupation.

After being taken to the outskirts of the city, forced to give up their valuables and remove their clothing by heavily armed German Troops and Ukrainian Police, they were led in groups to the bottom of a ravine called Babi-Yar, and one on top of another, shot in the back of the head. This is just one horrific example of what was befalling Jewish communities all across the German occupied Eastern territories.

Since the Soviet Union did not collapse under the weight of the massive German offensive in the opening weeks of the war the same way Poland and France had, and seemed to have a greater will to fight and much more resources than expected, the Germans needed to re-strategize for a longer campaign. The plan to resettle the East with ethnic Germans, to create a "human wall", which Hitler often talked about and even referred to in *Mein Kampf* (albeit further east after the Russians were forced to retreat over the Urals), must have taken on greater urgency.

Reichsführer-SS (Head of the SS, Hitler's security branch) Heinrich Himmler, the man overseeing this massive slaughter of Jews, was also in charge of the re-settlement program. The removal of the Jews and replacing them with Aryan settlers were inexorably linked. This explains Himmler's ramping up the Einsatzgruppen activities at this time and setting in motion plans to dispatch the hundreds of thousands of starving Jews herded in ghettos throughout Eastern Europe.

Bereft of any morality upon perpetrating these heinous acts of wanton murder in the east, it was now no longer a question for the Nazis what the "Final Solution to the Jewish Question" would be. The "resettlement plan" had unambiguously been replaced with extermination. In the fall of 1941, as soon as the "Final Solution" was determined, Jews from Western and Central Europe, already under siege since the Nazis had gained control, were expelled from their homes and brought east for their demise. Many of these Western Jews were brought to Lodz, further increasing the overcrowding and putting more strain on the limited food supply.

On December 20th, 1941, the German authorities demanded that the Judenrat Litzmannsdat select 20,000 Jews from the ghetto for "resettlement." Rumkowski saw this as an opportunity to rid the ghetto of all the criminals, his political enemies and those he deemed unproductive, but the demands for selection kept coming.

The Germans used deceit and violence to achieve compliance. Since the unemployed received a monthly stipend on which they depended for survival, the Germans simply announced a mandatory attendance at a certain time and place to continue receiving benefits. When the Jews arrived, they were just taken away. Those who did not, were eventually found, as everyone in the ghetto was registered by name, gender, birth date, address, country of origin, occupation, etc.

As if the insufferable daily hardships of ghetto life weren't enough, the Jews of Lodz had to now contend with a new, terrible reality: the constant, looming threat of deportation. The next large selection was of those not originally from Lodz. The ones that were still alive. Many had already succumbed to hunger and disease the brief time they were there.

In September 1942, they began to liquidate the hospitals. A cousin of Bubby's who was recovering from tuberculosis, managed to escape by crawling out a window. He could not have known at the time he would not be any safer elsewhere. The final selection, the most horrific, came next.

9

Aktion

September 5th, 1942. The sick, the elderly and children under the age of 10, were to be deported. In spite of a pleading, impassioned speech delivered by Rumkowski the day before imploring the ghetto inhabitants to cooperate, the Germans knew no one would ever willingly give up their children, so they surrounded the ghetto and confined everyone to their homes.

They came first at night, house to house. Initially it was the Jewish Police who were assigned to conduct the round-ups, Rumkowski preferring them over the ruthless Germans. However it was not going fast enough for the German authorities, so they took over the operation.

Later in life, when talking about the Holocaust, Bubby never mentioned the "Aktion" (German for "Operation"). It was too personal, too painful. One of her grandsons, having read of the event, curiously, innocently, yet in hindsight, insensitively, asked her about it. She stared at him, and in a voice with a seriousness he had never heard before asked, "How do you know about that?"

Her family should never know of and could never understand the terror, grief, helplessness, and despair she felt that endless week, hearing mothers driven to madness, their wailing children ripped from their arms. There were tears in Bubby's eyes as she revealed to him how often, late at night, when she was lying awake, alone, in a quiet house, she still heard their screams. Until then, the holocaust was something her grandson had only read about. It now became horrifyingly real.

"I don't know how those screams did not reach the heavens," she testified in the Fortunoff video. "Imagine," she said, her voice cracking, "babies, babies! We thought how can this be happening? Who could believe this, human beings doing this to human beings?"

Most mothers naturally worry over their children, but when Bubby had children of her own, she constantly feared for their lives. "My God," she thought, "What's going to happen to the babies? It's going to happen again!" She would stand over her children's cribs late into the night praying that nothing should happen to them. She truly believed they were in mortal danger until they reached the age of 10. At 10 they would be safe, at 10 they could work and be productive, at 10, no one would come for them. Bubby never let a baby in her presence cry and always saw to it they were comforted until calm. She had this persistent nightmare all her life of being cornered by the Germans with trucks and them jumping off and grabbing people off the street and throwing them in the back. Of all the suffering she experienced in the Holocaust, the Aktion was one of the most traumatic.

Many Holocaust survivors abandoned their faith. They could not reconcile how an all-powerful and benevolent God would allow such horrors and suffering. Bubby actually found faith after the war. It was no doubt a source of comfort, especially after losing her entire family, and provided purpose and meaning for raising a family of her own. After all her study and ruminations, however, she could not un-question one thing, "Why the children?"

During those terrible days in early September 1942, each household in the Lodz Ghetto was emptied out for inspection. People were forced to line up in rows of two and those that looked sick or weak were pulled out. Bubby always made sure to stand in the front row to not bear having to see if her parents were chosen. Not until she was a mother herself did it occur to her what her parents would have felt seeing her selected in front of them. Any family unwilling to give up a member was just taken entirely. Everyone had to be at the address where they were registered. Bubby's grandmother had been living with them at this time, so rather than put her family at risk, she went back to her apartment and was subsequently selected for deportation.

Bubby's father Abram, was 43, her mother Miriem 49, and after two plus years confined to the ghetto, she must have looked much older. She did not work in a factory and was officially registered as a homemaker. A neighbor advised her to tell the Germans when they asked her occupation, that she was a nurse. That advice saved her life during the Aktion as anyone not working, who looked old or did not have a profession considered useful, was deported

If the hunger, poverty, sickness, dehumanization, and dread of deportation weren't enough, the Germans terrorized the ghetto inhabitants by arbitrarily shooting them. A story rarely heard from Bubby was of how her Aunt was asked by a German soldier the age of her teenage son standing next to her. She proudly proclaimed his age, clearly exempting him from deportation, at which point the German casually drew his pistol and shot the young man in the face. Bubby said her Aunt (understandably), "Was never the same." after that.

When they came for her cousin who had fled home from the hospital, he told his parents not to worry. "I will get well," he assured them. "I am young and can work. The war will be over soon and we will all be together again". Traumatized by having their older son taken from them, they were not about to let this happen to their younger son who was within the age of selection and decided to hide together in a basement.

After the Aktion, Bubby and her parents went to check on them and learned of their fate from their neighbors. They were discovered, dragged out to the courtyard and beaten nearly to death before being taken away. This was Bubby's mother's youngest sister.

For a sense of the nightmare unfolding in the ghetto during the week of the Aktion, the following is an excerpt from Josef Zelkowicz's *In Those Terrible Days*.

What miserable, shocking and utterly illogical felicitations come in from the street. The mind does not accept them; the intellect cannot grasp them. Nevertheless, they are the absolute truth!

At 7 Zytnia Street...Now, how far away is Zytnia Street and how large is the whole ghetto? Just the same, just listen to the story that people from Zytnia Street are telling you, and believe it, even though it sounds so far away, so old, and so bizarre.

There, at 7 Zytnia Street, lived the wife of Dr. Zember - the Doctoress, the neighbors called her, even though only her husband, not she, was the doctor... He tried to escape from Dachau and was shot to death. They told her so, officially. They dispatched her from a small town to the ghetto along with her four-year old daughter, a little angel with fair hair and azure eyes. She lived at 7 Zytnia Street. They evicted her from her apartment, along with her little girl, for inspection in the courtyard.

41

She clutched her daughter's hand ...The two of them smiled at each other. The girl was pleased that her mother had taken her to the courtyard- after all, it was such a fine day in God's world, a day of soul-sustaining sunshine. Even her mother had to smile...After all, one had to show a merry face to prove that one was healthy and able bodied, not yet in need of being "thrown on the garbage heap..."

The girl's vigor, her pinkishness, flowing with blood and milk, caught his attention. As a loyal Party man, he could not let himself marvel at the beauty of a Jewish girl. As a loyal Party man he was born for one purpose only: to destroy everything Jewish. He made the decision he had to make: "Take that one." But the mother-no! She will not turn over the girl. As long as she lives, she will not let them tear her daughter from her. She continues to smile. What else can she do? To give him pleasure by showing her tears? To give him a free performance by allowing her face to express emotions...? She smiles and would not hand over the girl under any circumstances. He contorted his face into a spasm of mockery.

"Can it be so? She seriously intends to resist?"

Yes. Her smile did not at all interfere with her being a serious and devoted mother. She will not hand over her daughter! Let him do as he pleases...

He had been given a rather good upbringing. His chivalrous Junker school had taught him, instilled in him, the virtue of good

42

manners toward women. He just did not know whether this etiquette applied to Jewish women. He gave an embarrassed smile, and as he did so he pulled her and her daughter out of the line-up. The good school had won; its influence had not faded. So he gave her three minutes to think it over…three minutes by the clock.

The neighbors shuddered. Neighbors standing in the lengthy ranks sneaked a tearful look at the two of them, standing alone and smiling at each other-the girl in contentment for remaining with her mother who clutched her hand, and the mother in contentment for having her daughter next to her and within her…

Three minutes on the button, neither a second less nor a moment more. -So, what will it be? What has she decided?

She had nothing to decide. From her standpoint, nothing had changed during those three minutes: as long as she lives, she will not relinquish her daughter. Nothing changed; even the smile remained.

His smile, however, had become darker. More sinister. This may explain why he forgot the rules of good manners toward women and almost shouted as he issued his order:
"Face the wall…!
She faced the wall with the same smile on her face. She merely clasped her daughter's tiny palm with greater strength. Which explains why the girl raised her head toward her mother, probably in protest for the slight pain that the powerful grip was

43

causing her. However, the internal shift was just a secret between mother and daughter; outwardly, the mother showed no change. In contrast, the smile on his contorted face began to tremble perceptibly. He struggled to maintain that smile...But afterwards, when he brought both of them, mother and daughter, to the ground with two shots from his small handgun, the effort was no longer necessary; the smile on his contorted face was frozen in place. Had someone asked him why he was smiling and what the smile expressed - fear, cruelty, derangement - he might not have been aware that he was smiling at all and that a moment ago he had really murdered - quietly, politely, and "respectfully"- two people: the vibrant young woman and her four-year-old daughter next to her. Perhaps he would have shouted, at the moment of his action, the words that people will shout decades from now, when they read about these events. Perhaps he himself could have screamed, "It's a lie! A folly!"

But it really happened, however, unbelievable and illogical it was.

Bubby lived around the corner from Zytnia Street (Korngasse in Litzmannstadt). While lined up in her courtyard that beautiful September day, she would have heard those two gun shots.

Following the "Aktion," Rumkowski and his Judenrat were stripped of whatever limited autonomy they still had. The schools, hospitals, rabbinate, and other institutions were closed, and all cultural activities banned. Lodz was effectively turned into a work

44

camp, with nearly every remaining inhabitant now a slave laborer. There would be no more deportations for the next 22 months.

10

Chelmno

No one knew where the deportees were taken. Bubby never found out until after the war. In the ghetto and even later in the camps, she knew nothing of the gas chambers or the Einsatzgruppen murder squads. Who could even imagine such things? Maybe some of the adults had suspicions but Bubby was a sheltered teenager, she would have been shielded from any talk of such horrors. About 45 miles north of Lodz was a small town called Chelmno nad Nerem. It was there all the deportees were taken. None ever returned.

The Germans disguised their mass murder nearly as well as the brutal efficiency in which they conducted it. To control their victims and avoid panic, the Germans had to let them believe there was hope. After arriving at Chelmno, the people were brought to a large manor house where SS soldiers disguised as medics in white coats and even one posing as a friendly local squire wearing a traditional Bavarian hat with a feather in it, would inform them that they were being sent to work camps but must first bathe and have their clothing disinfected. They were told to remove any valuables and money that may be sown into the clothing lest it be destroyed during the steaming process and were given receipts to claim them afterwards.

A group of 50 to 80 people were then led down to the basement and along a brightly lit hallway with signs directing, "This way to the bathhouse." At the end was a ramp leading up to the open back of a cargo van. Before anyone knew what was happening, they were hurried up inside and the doors to the van quickly shut.

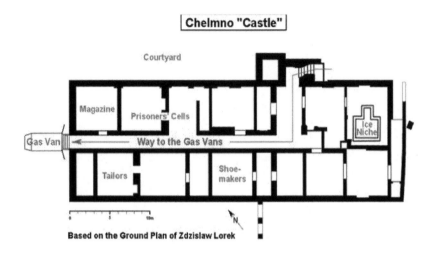

Chelmno "Castle"

Based on the Ground Plan of Zdzislaw Lorek

The proactive extermination of the Jews began with mass organized shootings by the Einsatzgruppen further east. Despite their indoctrination that the Jews were a sinister and subhuman race, the brutal, close range shooting of women and children was demoralizing, even for some of the staunchest Nazis, and many turned to alcoholism. After witnessing a mass execution and seeing the effects it was having on his soldiers, Heinrich Himmler ordered that more efficient methods separating them from the killing process be sought. They did not have to look far, as experts were already at hand with nearly two years of experience committing mass murder.

Before the Nazis were murdering Jews, they were "euthanizing" the mentally ill and physically disabled. This was called the T4 Program (named after their headquarters at 4 Tiergarten Street in Berlin). Initially, "patients" were killed

47

individually by lethal injection. This proved too costly and time consuming, so they began killing many at once with pure carbon monoxide released from cylinders into small, crowded rooms. They soon developed a mobile killing method, bringing the gas chambers to their victims in the form of hermetically sealed cargo vans sometimes disguised as moving or "Kaiser's Kaffe" (coffee) trucks. It was during the T4 Program that the Nazis honed the murderous techniques they would later apply at the death camps, even how to fool their victims of their fate just long enough to insure their orderly cooperation.

The Germans, always searching for more efficient and less costly methods to dispose of "Lebensunwertes Leben" (life unworthy of life), discovered that engine exhaust, which contains carbon monoxide, could be harnessed for this purpose and all it took were a few modifications to turn a vehicle into a self-contained, mobile gas chamber. A fleet of cargo vans were modified in Berlin to do just that and dispatched to all the Einsatzgruppen units. Arthur Greiser, the Nazi Governor responsible for the Warthegau (the conquered part of Western Poland annexed to the Reich) was eager to thin the ranks of Jews in his jurisdiction, especially now that more were being deported in from Central and Western Europe, so he requisitioned a few of these vans and set them up at Chelmno.

Once the van doors were shut, the driver connected a hose to the exhaust, donned a gas mask and started the engine. It took about 20 minutes until all the screams stopped. In Chelmno, as the bodies could not be disposed of in town, they were driven 2.5 miles up the

48

road to a remote clearing in a forest hidden by a tall wooden fence. There a group of Jewish men selected from an earlier transport, chained together at the ankles so they could not escape, were forced to remove the bodies from the vans and bury them in mass graves. Later, as the stench of decomposing corpses began to permeate the countryside and reach nearby villages, they started burning the bodies on pyres. To conceal these crimes against humanity, the previously buried bodies were exhumed and cremated, their bones crushed and dumped in the nearby Ner river at night.

After being cleaned of all the vomit, excrement, and blood, the vans were driven back to the manor house for another load of victims. This process was repeated seven to eight times a day with each of the two to three vans.

11

Survival

After the Aktion, there were around 80,000 inhabitants left in the ghetto. Things settled into a routine with over 90% of the population working. The few children and elderly remaining were immediate family of the Jundenrat and Ghetto Police. They were exempted from deportation to ensure the participation of their relatives in the round-ups.

The Lodz Ghetto was a source of cheap and skilled labor for the German war machine. When hundreds of other Jewish ghettos in Poland and beyond were liquidated by the end of 1943, their inhabitants sent to their deaths at Treblinka, Belzec, Sobibor, Majdanek or Auschwitz-Birkenau, shot or gassed in vans, Lodz alone remained. The Germans, having no intention of allowing the Jews of Lodz to survive beyond what they could squeeze out of them, provided only one loaf of bread per worker, per week.

Though the ghetto was completely sealed from the outside world, news still managed to trickle in. By 1944, the German army was on the defensive and many dared hope that if they could just hold out a little longer, they would survive. That June, however, the deportations began again. The decision to finally liquidate the Lodz ghetto had been made and the killing center of Chelmno reopened. At first the Germans asked for volunteers, saying they would be sent to work in Germany. Considering there had not been a deportation for nearly two years and laborers must be needed for the war effort, some volunteered, possibly believing, hoping it was true. Bubby's father likely knew better, but volunteered that July nonetheless. "Let's not destroy the family yet," he told Bubby and her mother. "Let me go myself. The war will be over soon and I'll come back so we can still have a family."

Abram Pinkus was not just a smart man, he was a pragmatist. He probably knew he was not coming back. He had done all he could to help support his family the past four and a half years, and felt there was nothing more he could do and that he might even be a liability. As an adult male, he required more calories than his wife and daughter to survive and did not want to burden them. He had witnessed over the years in the ghetto countless families destroyed, dragged down by a member they suffered to try and save. Bubby, who looked up to and adored her father, would not have questioned his judgment to leave and believed he would return. In fact, one of the things that enabled her to hold on, especially during those horrendous last few months of the war spent in the camps, when even the strongest succumbed, was the hope of seeing him again.

"My father wasn't afraid of anything," she would say in admiration. "Except the Germans." Later in life, in the quiet moments, Bubby must have ruminated over her father's decision to leave her and her mother. She never shared the realization she must have come to, the thought of him sacrificing himself for her was too much to bear. There were some things Bubby kept deep down and entirely to herself, this must have been one of them.

On July 15th the deportations to Chelmno suddenly stopped. The respite was short lived as the Germans merely decided to change the destination. They realized they could eliminate the Jews of Lodz much faster by sending them to a facility located about 140 miles south.

12

Liquidation

In August of 1944, just a few weeks before Bubby's 19th birthday, the final liquidation of the Lodz ghetto began. To try and make this last deportation go as smoothly as possible, the Germans promulgated the lie that everyone was being evacuated west to work camps in Germany. This was grounded in some truth. On June 23, 1944, the Soviet Red Army launched Operation Bagration. By August 19, they had retaken vast amounts of territory all the way to the outskirts of Warsaw and destroyed most of the Wehrmacht's vaunted Army Group Centre.

After suffering massive losses at the hands of the Wehrmacht, Stalin and his STAVKA (Soviet Military High Command), had learned from their mistakes and were now giving the Germans a taste of their own medicine. Deceiving the Germans as to when and where they would attack and effectively coordinating air, armor, artillery and infantry in conjunction with partisan operations disrupting communications and supply lines in the rear, they had inflicted the largest defeat on the German Army since Stalingrad.

The faint thunder of distant artillery and ever more present wail of air raid sirens confirmed to the ghetto inhabitants that the Russians were in fact coming. The Germans took advantage of these circumstances to reinforce their lie, assuring workers they would be following their factories' dismantled machinery loaded onto trains heading west away from the advancing front. Even those that did not believe a word they were told and knew better, were too starving and exhausted to resist and thought things could not possibly be worse elsewhere. Some tried hiding hoping they could hold out until the Russians arrived, though most were eventually discovered by the constant sweeps, or caught venturing out for food.

So relatively orderly, over the course of three weeks, most of the remaining 70,000 or so Jews still alive in Lodz gathered at the central prison and other designated assembly areas and marched in groups of 5,000 to the train station for "resettlement", Rumkowski and his family included. The night before their deportation, Bubby and her mother slept on the prison floor.

Upon arriving at the station, Bubby sensed something was very wrong. Instead of regular passenger cars with seats and windows, they were being loaded into cattle cars. Bubby and her mother were crammed in a car with nearly 100 other people. Some of the few remaining children in the ghetto were in the car with them. Bubby recalled a mother clutching her infant (born after the Aktion), weeping inconsolably.

"Why are you crying?" They tried comforting her, "We're going to a labor camp. It will be better there."

"We're not going to a labor camp." She sobbed back at them matter-of-factly. "This is the end."

"How do you know that?"

"I just do." She responded. "I feel it."

Some people's instincts were correct, Bubby observed, especially mothers.

The busy railways in Poland carrying soldiers and supplies back and forth to the front took priority over all other trains, especially ones loaded with Jews. What would otherwise be a few hour trip took much longer. Bubby and her mother traveled, given no food or water, for three days. This is an experience she never, ever talked about, which is a sure indication of how horrendous it must have been. The confinement, stench, and stifling heat Bubby endured, especially when her train stopped for hours in the hot August sun, is unimaginable. Many died en route, their rotting corpses crushed against the living.

When they finally arrived at their destination, Bubby was too short to see out the gaps in the wood slats at the top of the car, but noticed the reaction of one of the men next to her. He was a Jewish policeman and as he stared outside his hands began to shake. He knew where they were and what that meant.

13

Auschwitz

By mid-1944, the death camp at Auschwitz-Birkenau was running at full capacity "processing" over 6,000 people a day. Trainloads of Jews from Hungary would arrive one after another. Nearly 400,000 Hungarian Jews were murdered at Auschwitz from May to July. Now, the last remaining Jews of Poland (of which nearly three million had already been killed), the Jews of Lodz, were next.

The Lodz Jews looked different than the Hungarian Jews. The Hungarians had not suffered long in ghettos, their clothing and bodies not yet ruined. In contrast, the Jews from Lodz, confined in their ghetto for over 4 years surviving on next to nothing, were skin and bones under their loosely fitting, tattered attire. Bubby, however, was strong willed and extremely disciplined. She would carefully stretch out her rations and took care of her personal hygiene as best she could, washing her hair with water cupped in her hands. She did not look nearly as emaciated as most of the other Lodz Jews and people were surprised when she told them where she was from.

The doors of Bubby's train were thrust open and men in striped uniforms with shaved heads who did not look malnourished (and some, Bubby thought, not Jewish), began hurrying them off.

"See." They said to each other, their worst fears momentarily allayed, "They all look well. This must be a work camp."

Bubby remembered while getting off the train, being struck by an odd exchange. A woman was gathering her clothes off the floor when one of the prisoners said to her in Yiddish, "Don't worry about the little things, just save your life". At the time, Bubby did not understand what he meant by that.

The men and women with children were separated into long columns five rows deep each and moved slowly forward in front of a German SS officer who with a simple gesture was sending most to the right and some to the left. Bubby will never forget the handsome, impeccably groomed, uniformed gentleman with white gloves making the selections. She would later learn that this was none other than Joseph Mengele, the "Doctor of Death" himself.

All the children, the elderly and anyone who appeared weak, ill, or unfit to work would be sent right. Young mothers were encouraged by the escorting prisoners and at times even the guards, to hand over their children to the older women. There were told they would be reunited soon. Nearly all refused and went with their children. On the platform, Bubby was sent left, her mother right. No one being selected knew or dared imagine what the selections meant. Bubby was told the older people were just being sent to a separate camp, "the other side" they called it. Bubby thought, "My poor mother, let her at least have my bread." So as her mother was being led away, Bubby threw her the half loaf she had been saving. She never had a chance to say goodbye and never saw her again.

Unlike the vans of Chelmno and the Einsatzgruppen, or the gas chambers of the Operation Reinhard death camps (named in honor of Reinhard Heydrich, a high ranking SS officer and one of the main architects of the Holocaust, who was assassinated in Prague, Czechoslovakia in the spring of 1942 by British SOE-trained Czech and Slovak soldiers-in-exile parachuted back into their homeland under Operation Anthropoid) at Treblinka, Belzec and Sobibor which piped in carbon monoxide exhaust from captured Soviet, diesel tank engines to kill their victims, Auschwitz-Birkenau used a cyanide based pesticide called Zyklon B. This poison came in the form of crystalized pellets that turned to gas when exposed to air. This was a much more efficient method of mass murder and the Germans were all about efficiency.

Bubby's mother, along with up to 1,000 or more victims were led down to an underground room and told to undress for disinfection and showers. They were then quickly herded into another room with dummy overhead shower nozzles, a ruse to reinforce the lie and try and forestall panic until everyone was crammed inside and the doors sealed shut. Soon after, Zyklon B pellets were poured into the room from overhead vent shafts outside by gloved Nazi SS Officers in gas masks. Death could take anywhere from 2 to 20 painful minutes depending on where one was situated and temperature in the room. Engines were revved nearby to mask the terrifying screams. As soon as there was silence, fans were switched on to ventilate the room and the Sonderkommando (groups of Jewish prisoners forced into handling the bodies) wearing boots, gloves and gas masks would enter and remove the dead for incineration in the crematorium above. The morbidly efficient Germans had the Sonderkommando harvest anything of value from the corpses before cremation. Teeth with gold fillings were pulled and heads shaved for their hair. The Nazis' preferred method of extermination even saved them from having to disinfect the hair as Zyklon B gas also killed head lice.

At the Auschwitz slaughter factory, disposing the bodies, the evidence of mass murder, had the crematoria ovens running day and night. The Germans developed a system for the Sonderkommando to stack different sized bodies (adults and small children) in various positions to burn as many at once as possible with little or no accelerant. The ovens would get so hot, flames would spew high out of the smoke stacks. One of the male prisoners who liked a young woman Bubby was friends with, once saw them staring at the smoke stacks in the distance. He told them not to worry, that their families were fine on "the other side" and he would send regards to their mothers. They believed him because they wanted to believe him. "I was an only child." Bubby said. "My mother was the world to me."

Bubby was overwhelmed and confused by this massive camp and did not understand where she was or what she was doing there. Her group was marched past what seemed like endless rows of barracks to one with showers and were ordered to strip naked. They were given no soap and there was a horrible odor in the water; a disinfectant. Their heads were shaven and they were issued gray prison dresses and wooden shoes. The guards would shout orders at them the whole time. They laughed and cursed at them in German, "Fafluchta Juden" (Filthy Jews).

Unlike other survivors of Auschwitz, Bubby does not have a number tattooed on her forearm. She always told us it was because by that time, later in the war, they stopped tattooing. The fact is, prisoners who were not selected for the gas chambers upon arrival were still being tattooed until the very end. Since 1941, tattoos were how the slaves at Auschwitz were identified and the Germans would never shirk on their established means of record keeping.

Of the 67,000 or so arrivals from Lodz to Auschwitz in August of 1944, 45,000 were immediately gassed and cremated, 3,000 were tattooed with serial numbers and sent to work and 19,000 were kept in "reserve." At this point in the war, Germany was in such desperate need for labor they had to draw from the ranks of Jews who would have otherwise been exterminated. Though Bubby was young and at the time of her arrival at Auschwitz in fair health, she was petite, not a top candidate for hard manual labor, so rather than being sent straight to a labor camp she was kept in limbo, her fate to be determined over the next few days. Bubby's lack of a tattoo is a testament to how close to death she actually came.

Bubby was assigned to Block 26 of Auschwitz-Birkenau II. These bunks, formally occupied by the last remaining Gypsies of Auschwitz, some 4,000 or so, were made vacant when they were all gassed and cremated shortly before Bubby's arrival. Seven to eight women were assigned to each wooden planked bunk bed, no mattresses, no blankets. What little warmth they got was from each other. It was here she recalled for the first time the film "Dante's Inferno" she saw as a girl. This is what hell must be like. It was surreal. Wild people running around. She noticed how the non-Jewish Polish prisoners seemed to have more freedom in the camp. The Blockältester (the Polish woman prisoner in charge of her Block) suggested the women prostitute themselves to get more food.

"You could get whatever you want here in Auschwitz," she told them. "But only from men. If I ever catch you with one though, you'll be shot." She added.

The female Kapos (guards who were themselves prisoners) wore the finest clothing from Belgium and France gifted to them by their prisoner boyfriends, taken from women who were gassed and cremated. The Kapos were even crueler than the Germans.

"We suffered so much when we first came here," they would say. "Why should you have it easier?"

No food was given to them that first day. Bubby and some of the other women thought to stop eating altogether so they would just

62

die and be free of this nightmare. She would soon learn however a body's will to survive is deep and primal, overpowering all other conscious thought. They could not not eat. When they were finally given some watery soup, a calm seemed to fall over them. No one was crying anymore or missed their families, they became like different people. Bubby and others suspected the soup was drugged with some kind of tranquilizer. They were probably correct. The Germans used their concentration camp inmates as guinea pigs, conducting all sorts of horrific medical experiments on them and unwitting pharmaceutical trials. Drugging their prisoners with mood stabilizers to keep them docile was likely just another means of control, as well as to observe the effects.

The Germans for a time even handed out to their soldiers and airmen methamphetamine to increase their alertness, enhance their morale and enable them to go for days without sleep. Some say this was one of the reasons for the success of Blitzkrieg, the Wehrmacht's rapid victories early in the war.

A typical day at Auschwitz started with roll call at 5am. They had to stand at attention for inspection, sometimes for hours. Even though it was still August, early mornings in Poland could get very cold. Those who could not get out of bed or stand in line were beaten and dragged away. Those who looked ill or too weak were pulled out of the line-ups. This "appell" (roll call) was repeated in the evening.

"God help us if anyone was missing," Bubby would say.

People began to be randomly selected for no apparent reason. No one knew where they were going or if it was better or worse to be selected. Breakfast every day consisted of lukewarm, black ersatz coffee and a slice of stale bread. For dinner, a bowl of soup. Bubby actually appreciated the meager rations at Auschwitz. It was more food than she had received on a daily basis in Lodz.

Bubby made a conscious effort to reach out and act kindly to the middle-aged women in her bunk. She hoped by doing so, somehow, in some way, her mother would also be treated well wherever she was. Bubby had a feeling she might be gone, that she could not survive their separation in her condition. She took some solemn comfort though, that her mother no longer had to witness her daughter's suffering or she hers. This is one of the reasons Bubby never discussed the Holocaust with her children (she did not even want them to read or hear about it), even when they were much older. She did not want them to anguish over their mother's suffering the way she had.

Bubby was in Auschwitz-Birkenau for 12 days until she and a group of women were selected, for what and where they did not know. With SS guards screaming (they were always screaming at them Bubby said), their German Shepherds lunging on their leashes, viscously snapping and barking, the women, running to avoid being bitten, were herded onto a train. Bubby could never have imagined what lay ahead and that the worst was yet to come.

14

Bergen-Belsen

Located in Northern Germany, Bergen-Belsen was built in 1937 to house workers constructing a nearby military base. After the start of World War II, the huts there were used to house prisoners of war and over the next few years the camp was expanded to accommodate many more.

In April of 1943, the SS commandeered part of Bergen-Belsen turning it into a "holding" camp for Jews with citizenship from neutral and some Western European countries. These Jews were to be used as prisoner exchanges for German nationals being held in internment camps abroad or ransomed for hard currency, raw material, or supplies. Their treatment was initially much better than Jews in other camps due to their perceived potential exchange value, though many were still forced to work in a shoe factory at the camp, repurposing shoe leather brought in from all parts of occupied Europe.

Starting in late August of 1944, Jews from concentration camps back east were being brought to Bergen-Belsen for use as slave labor at the nearby armament factories under construction. Bubby was sent to a new section of the camp housing women. At first it was a much cleaner camp and they even had straw for beds. Bubby remembers seeing families from Hungary in an adjacent camp. She found it strange that there were intact families there, not in prison clothes, who appeared to be in good health. She could not have known then that Heinrich Himmler himself took some of the last remaining, unsullied Jews left in Europe, those from Budapest, as hostages for negotiating with the allies. He had nearly 1,700 Jews sent to their own camp at Bergen-Belsen, where they were treated relatively well. Such was not to be the case for Bubby, and in the next few months, as the war neared its inglorious end, for no one else at Bergen-Belsen.

The boredom of those first few weeks with no work and nothing to pass the time was torturous. Bubby fell ill and was sent to the infirmary called the Kraken Stuber where there was no medicine or even food. Being relegated to the "infirmary" was essentially a death sentence. Part of Bergen-Belsen had been re-designated as a "recovery" camp, where prisoners from other concentration camps too sick to work were brought. "Recovery" was a euphemism, as no medical care was provided, and the living conditions were horrendous. It was set up to segregate those who could not work, essentially to die.

Bubby remembers families would come and share what little they had with their sick relatives. Despite the conditions there, Bubby managed to get better and return to her bunk. She then almost welcomed being selected to work in a munitions factory at one of Bergen-Belsen's sub camps near the town of Unterluss.

There Bubby endured the hardest physical labor in her life. They were forced to pull trees out of the ground and run, always run, with loaded wagons back and forth. To Bubby, the work seemed pointless, intended to just torture them. Though the Germans did need forest cleared in the area for a testing site, her instincts were not off the mark as the Nazis had a policy of "extermination through work." After long grueling days, in the barracks at night, Bubby remembers the women with good voices would sing, often in Hebrew. Many of them were Zionists and likely sang the "Hatikva" (currently the national anthem of the state of Israel), a song of hope and pride.

The female German guards in the camp, Bubby would say, were the worst, extremely cruel. They walked around with crop whips, constantly lashing out with them at any opportunity. If your bed was not made absolutely perfect for example, you were whipped. As a child, Bubby was always well-behaved and obedient and now, with the Germans, even more so. You were always told to just follow orders and nothing would happen to you. Bubby kept her head down and avoided the Germans as much as possible. Even then however, it wasn't always enough.

One day in the middle of the camp they were handing out soup and as Bubby was walking away with her portion, suddenly, out of nowhere, she felt large, heavy leather gloved hand cover her mouth, violently spin her around and slap her to the ground. She was so shocked she did not even cry out. She had no idea what she could have done. Her friends told her later how they watched helplessly in horror as it unfolded, seeing the guard race up behind her from a distance, their cries of warning caught in their throats, instinctively terrified at uttering a sound to suffer the consequences. Fortunately, someone nearby shouted that he had mistaken Bubby for someone else and they left her alone. Bubby would often wonder how she survived the camps and thought her obedience one of the reasons. Another was the simple pleasure she took from the warmth of the sun which she craved so badly, taking any opportunity she could to soak it up while clinging to her filthy blanket.

Amidst all the madness and sadism of the concentration camps, there was some humanity. An older SS guard assigned to watch them work would often pretend to be sleeping so the women could rest. A younger SS guard fell in love with a beautiful Hungarian Jewess and consequently acted kindly to the other women. He was handsome, and the women could not help but flirt. One day he and the Hungarian girl were gone. Bubby heard they ran away together, but were soon caught and shot dead in the forest. This was one of the stories heard often from Bubby. Maybe because to her, it exemplified the tragedy of the Holocaust: youth, love and hope callously snuffed out.

Winter came and their forced marches were now through snow. Some of the girls' toes, after turning black, would fall off from frostbite. Bubby got sick again. On one of the marches she was unable to keep up. Anyone who fell behind was beaten, shot, or just left to die. It was night and snowing hard. Bubby didn't have the strength to walk anymore and lost sight of her group. She lay down in the falling snow and quietly surrendered. As she began to drift off to sleep and death from hypothermia, she was jostled awake. One of the women in her group came back for her.

"Leave me." Bubby said, "I don't even know where to go."

"You can't stay here." The woman pleaded, "You'll freeze to death."

She then sat down next to Bubby. After staying there together for a while quietly in the snow, Bubby, not wanting her friend to share her fate, decided she would try and get up. They slowly began walking through the blizzard, Bubby being practically carried. After some time, by some miracle, they saw the lights of the camp. Bubby recalled her friend who saved her, "She was a very simple woman with a wonderful heart.... She died before liberation."

Bubby would never forget her name. It was Bella, which means beautiful.

15

Liberation

As the Germans retreated from Poland, they took all the prisoners they could use for slave labor and/or as hostages with them. In January of 1945, they abandoned Auschwitz, "death" marching 60,000 prisoners over 40 miles to towns with transit hubs, then herding them onto "Holocaust Trains" for dispersal to various concentration and forced labor camps in Germany. Many did not survive the trip.

Bergen-Belsen, originally designed to accommodate no more than 15,000 prisoners, by early 1945, had swelled to over 50,000 with more constantly arriving. In these overcrowded and consequently unsanitary conditions, a typhus epidemic broke out.

Typhus is an infectious bacterial disease spread by body lice and Bergen-Belsen was infested. Untreated, especially to the malnourished and those suffering from other diseases, such as tuberculosis and dysentery, typhus is extremely lethal. By March of 1945 nearly 600 people a day were dying in the camp, Anne Frank, and her sister Margot among them.

As Bergen-Belsen was not an extermination camp there were no methods in place for disposing vast amounts of bodies, so they literally began to pile up. Bubby compared these last horrible weeks to the frightening hell scene from the 1935 movie "Dante's Inferno", mounds of naked bodies writhing in agony.

She recalled her indifference to the endless corpses strewn about and being uncomfortably aware that what she should be feeling was horror and revulsion. Later in life, Bubby would come to understand that her lack of emotion was normal. She would often quote from the book, *Man's Search for Meaning* by the notable Viennese Jewish Psychiatrist and Holocaust Survivor Viktor Frankl, "Abnormal behavior in abnormal situations is normal."

Afflicted with typhus, Bubby was back in the Kraken Stuber. One day, the Germans came in and announced that all those who had been there a while should make room for new arrivals. Bubby, fearing that if she stayed, she would be shot, volunteered to leave. She was so sick she could barely move. Just to get down the few steps from the barracks she had to lift each leg with her arms.

Wandering outside clutching her lice infested blanket she was directed by some prisoners to a bunk with other terminally ill women. There she found people that looked like skeletons scattered across the floor. One of them was a young teenage girl completely naked. She begged Bubby to cover her. Bubby draped her blanket over her and huddled with her for warmth. When she awoke the next day, the girl, still clinging to her, was dead.

God only knows how many days Bubby remained lying on that floor, with no food or water. She has been pushed aside into a corner and left for dead. Her legs were swollen and her eyes crusted shut by the hardened puss that oozed from her open sores. All Bubby remembers thinking at that time was thank God her mother did not have to see her like this. Drifting in and out of consciousness, she must have been moments from death. Suddenly she became alert, something was different. The routine sounds of the camp, the shuffling murmurs occasionally punctuated by the drone of bombers high overhead, became silent.

"Am I finally dead?" Bubby thought.

She heard faint noises of a commotion in the distance and then young women just outside her window shouting excitedly, "The British are here!"

"Oh these poor girls," she thought, "They've finally lost their minds."

For the last five and a half years, which to that point comprised nearly a third of her cognitive life, Bubby had known nothing but war and suffering. It was understandable she couldn't conceive of anything else and couldn't believe they were finally being liberated.

With the relentless allied strategic bombing of Germany, infrastructure to the area was damaged and the camp lost running water. The Germans did not bother fixing it, nor tried to secure other means of supplying water for their prisoners, so the already abject conditions in the camp got exponentially worse. Fearing that the advancing British Army would overrun them and spread typhus into the countryside, the Germans surrendered the camp and agreed to create a neutral zone around it.

On April 15th, 1945, advance units from the 63rd anti-tank regiment of the British Army entered Bergen-Belsen. Though battle-hardened, nothing could have prepared these soldiers for what they encountered.

Bubby remembered a voice in a strange accent call out in German, "Is anyone alive?" She then heard footsteps approach and felt her blanket slowly peeled back. She managed to force open her eyes partially to see a man in a uniform that was not German standing over her. Bubby was confused, she had never seen this man before.

"Who are you?" She managed to utter, "What are you talking about?"

"The war is over," he said. "I'm not going to let you die," he then assured her. "You are too young."

Carefully, he cradled her up and carried her to a field hospital hastily set up in a bunk at the camp. She was soon moved to the nearby former regional German Army Headquarters building called the "Rundhaus" (Round House), named for its unique half round façade, which was converted to a makeshift medical facility.

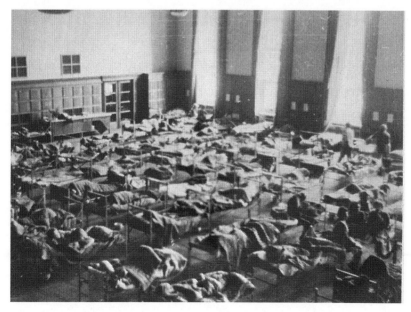

Over the next couple of weeks, this soldier that found her, took a personal interest in seeing that Bubby received proper medical treatment and came every day to check on her until she was stable.

After witnessing so much suffering and death and feeling helpless to do anything about it, saving Bubby, just one life, must have given him some solace.

Despite the best efforts of the British to care for them, the condition of the Bergen-Belsen survivors upon liberation was so poor that over the next few weeks, an additional 14,000 died. Had it not been for this lone British soldier who found her and then looked after her, Bubby would no doubt have been one of them. She never knew this soldier's name but would never forget his kindness.

Medical students arrived from Belgium to treat the hospitalized survivors along with nuns as nurses. Bubby could hear them giving out diagnoses, she was "Polish Jewish Critical." They tried in vain to give her fluids intravenously and she developed an abscess. As other patients slowly began to be released to displaced persons camps, Bubby was still too sick to move.

All the well laid plans of the Third Reich were rapidly unraveling. On April 30th, 1945, with the Russians ferociously fighting their way to the center of Berlin, Adolf Hitler, in his private bunker under the Reich's Chancellery along with his newly wed wife Eva Braun, committed suicide.

They could have gotten away with it. Much of the evidence of the Nazi genocide had been eradicated. As early as 1942, most of the mass graves of over 1.2 million Jewish victims of the Einsatzgruppen were dug up and the bodies cremated.

In November of 1943, nearly all traces of the three death camps of Operation Reinhard where over 1.5 million Jews were murdered, Belzec, Sobibor and Treblinka, were destroyed and all the killing vans stripped down for parts. Later in the war, as the allies slowly surrounded Germany, the Nazis made sure to burn most of the meticulous records they kept on their crimes.

Ironic how it was Bergen-Belsen in the end, a holding camp deep inside Germany where there were never any gas chambers and where the prisoners were initially treated relatively better compared to all the other concentration camps, would be the one that exposed the horrors of the Holocaust to the world, as in the waning months of the war, it turned into a horrific death camp of its own.

The British, after clearing the camp of survivors, documenting the atrocities in pictures and film and forcing the SS and Hungarian guards along with German civilians from surrounding villages to bury the bodies, burned the entire typhus infected camp to the ground.

16

Malmo

Once Bubby was stable, and as soon as the war in Europe was officially over in May of 1945, she was offered to go with other survivors to Malmo, Sweden for recuperation. She was initially hesitant to sign up, worried that her father and mother, if they were still alive, would not know where she went. She then realized, as their only child and "apple of their eye," they would keep looking until they found her. If they did not, they must be gone.

She did not recall how she traveled to Sweden. She remembered fainting upon arrival and then waking up in the hospital in Malmo. She was kept in isolation for three months. Her scabies infection was so bad, they needed to scrub off all her skin from head to toe with a hard-bristled brush. It took a lot of treatment, medicine and time for the scabies to be cured.

The first time she got up on her own was to the ladies' room and she was startled to find a man there. It took Bubby a moment to realize, having not seen a mirror in over a year, she was looking at her own reflection. She did not recognize herself, entirely bald, gaunt and with yellow skin.

The Swedes were wonderful. Many volunteers came by to help feed and care for her and the other recovering survivors. It had been many years since Bubby experienced kindness and it no doubt helped restore her faith in humankind. Bubby needed physical therapy to regain some of her normal motor function and ability to walk properly.

Later in life, her children would sometimes hear Bubby say, "If you don't use it, you lose it." When asked what she meant, she explained how after the war she was so far gone, she could not even walk. In the hospital she would hold onto the wall and drag herself across the room until she could use her legs again.

When they were ready to leave the hospital, the Swedes moved them to a specially built camp to complete their rehabilitation and quarantine them in case they still had any lingering contagions. The camp was laid out with barracks in neat rows and Bubby and the other survivors thought they had been tricked. The Swedes later realized it was an insensitive mistake to build their recovery camp like a Nazi concentration one.

After Bubby recuperated, she remained in Malmo with other survivors in a DP (Displaced Persons) camp. Up until that point, everything was simply about survival. In the ghetto and camps there had been no time to think of anything else. Now, after her physical recovery, the psychological recovery began. As Bubby and the other survivors learned what happened to their family and friends and what it meant to go to the "other side," a terrible depression set in.

"How is it that we survived when so many wonderful people did not?" Bubby struggled with survivors' guilt, a symptom of post-traumatic stress disorder. Another tragedy of the Holocaust, with entire communities and families wiped out, those few that survived, had to grieve alone.

She remembered they brought in a couple of Rabbis to say a prayer with them. Most of the survivors there did not come from religious homes, but the moment the Rabbis began to utter the first Hebrew words, they all broke down in tears. For years they were not allowed any freedom of expression or religion and now, out in the open, they were able to pray. This really helped begin the healing process, Bubby said.

Whether aware of it or not, Bubby had an extraordinary innate strength and a tremendous will to live. She persevered and courageously chose life.

17

Marriage

Of the few hundred people at the DP camp there were only a handful of men. Abe Schultz (Zaidey) was one of them. Not much is known about Zaidey before or during the war. We know he came from an Orthodox Hasidic family, coincidently, from a small town near Lodz.

When the Germans invaded, he fled east to the city of Lvov only to be deported shortly after, along with over a million other Poles, by the Soviets after they occupied Eastern Poland. He suffered two years in a Siberian prison camp until he and the other surviving Poles (nearly half had died in captivity), were granted amnesty shortly after Germany's invasion of the Soviet Union.

Traveling with the newly formed Polish Anders Army (Menachem Begin, a future Prime Minister of Israel, was one of their Jewish recruits), along with thousands of other civilians to Iran, Zaidey somehow managed to flee to neutral Turkey, where he stayed on the run for the duration of the war. Upon returning home and finding his community decimated, he learned that his younger brother, the sole survivor out of six siblings, somehow made it to Sweden. The story goes he snuck on a ship in Lubeck, Germany and after being discovered by the crew, threatened to jump overboard and swim. They let him stay.

He must have fallen in love with Bubby at first sight as out of all the women in the camp, he chose her. Bubby initially rejected his courtship, though if any one remembers Zaidey, he was nothing if not persistent. While some of the other Jewish girls there were marrying Swedes, Bubby never for a moment considered marrying outside her faith. As a pretty young teenager back in Lodz, her friends would tell her she could marry a German, which at that time was considered a huge compliment as the educated Poles very much admired the Germans and their culture, but her father would say if she ever came home with a Goy (Gentile) "I'll break his legs." Though he was a secular Jew and raised his daughter to be enlightened, he clearly drew the line when it came to intermarriage and Bubby deeply respected him so respected that.

Bubby and Zaidey married in August of 1947. They had two boys Daniel (Danny) and Shia (Freddy). Life in Sweden was idyllic and safe. Bubby would say how no one ever locked their doors and how when she went to the supermarket, all the mothers, including her, would leave their babies in their carriages outside.

Zaidey wanted to leave Sweden in order to raise the boys as Orthodox Jews. As Zaidey's brother was already living in New York, they were able to obtain visas. So, on January 10th, 1952, with Bubby eight months pregnant with her third child Miriam, they arrived in the United States.

18

America

Living in Brooklyn, New York, they were part of a large Orthodox Jewish community. In a brief time, they established themselves and Zaidey opened a successful garment business. Bubby would do his books. They had their fourth child Michelle.

In 1969, their son Shia (Freddy) left to study at the Diaspora Yeshiva in Jerusalem, Israel. Bubby and Zaidey went to visit him. It was their first time in Israel and Bubby used the opportunity to see her first cousin, Karl, a doctor living in Haifa, her only relative to survive the Holocaust.

All these years Bubby never had a chance to truly share her grief. Though she spoke and opened up to her husband who could certainly relate to her loss of family and even some of her suffering, as he had spent two years in a Soviet gulag, there was no way he could fully appreciate what she had endured. She never spoke about the Holocaust with anyone else until she was much older, and all her children were grown. She used to say that it was impossible to truly convey what had happened to anyone who did not live through it so why bother talking about it.

Her cousin Karl though, had experienced everything she had: the ghetto, starvation, humiliation, Holocaust trains, Auschwitz, forced labor and death marches. He was also family. When they met, after not seeing one another for over 20 years, neither spoke a word, they just sat together, held each other's hands and cried.

For her last 50 years or so, Bubby lived in comfortable yet modest little row house in Canarsie, Brooklyn. Even as the neighborhood gradually changed from mostly Jews to immigrants from the Caribbean, Bubby happily stayed. Her mailman, a Haitian immigrant, once asked her if she was a Holocaust survivor. No doubt because of her age and thick Polish accent but she none the less asked how he knew. His answer surprised her.

"I see it in your eyes," he said.

Her bright, pale blue eyes always sparkled with energy, but I guess some also saw the sadness. Bubby was always optimistic and full of life and never for a moment wallowed in self-pity. She would just sometimes matter-of-factly say, "I had a wonderful childhood, but they took my youth."

Though Bubby was a strictly Orthodox Jewish woman, she loved the melting pot which is New York City and embraced all races and cultures. She cherished her daughter-in-law, a convert to Judaism from Guyana and totally spoiled her 14 biracial grandchildren. For decades, she did the books for a nursing home owned by immigrants from India and had a wonderful relationship with them. She worked there full-time until she was 85, commuting every day by public bus.

After she retired, she still lived independently, checked on daily by her doting daughters. She had energy and all her wits, and

84

got around with the help of a walking stick she made from a broom handle.

Bubby, more than anyone, was aware of the dangers of prejudice. She would always say, which confounded almost everyone who heard it, that the Holocaust could happen again, even in America. She knew firsthand that with any form of discrimination comes the inherent danger of a political party promoting it and if that party comes to full power, legislatively sanctioning it and then, under the cover of war, the potential for wholesale pilferage, enslavement, torture, and genocide. Not so inconceivable when one learns that acts of genocide have already occurred since the Holocaust, in Cambodia, Rwanda, Bosnia, Darfur and even in this century to the Yazidis by ISIS.

Bubby would often wonder why she survived. Her family and all of us privileged to have known her can easily provide the answer. Thank you, Bubby, for your love, your strength, your inspiration and your hope.

We will never forget.

Conclusion

Of the approximately 200,000 Jews who passed through the Lodz ghetto, only around 7,000, less than 4%, survived the war. The war cost the lives of over 6 million Polish citizens, half of them Jews. Over 90% of the entire Jewish population of Poland was murdered in the Holocaust. Today there are only around 3,000 Jews still living in Poland, 0.1% of the pre-war population.

Few events in modern history are studied as broadly as the Holocaust. Holocaust historians are usually put into one of two groups, Intentionalists and Functionalists. The Intentionalists contend, the Führer, Adolf Hitler, issued direct verbal orders to his closest and most loyal underlings (Himmler, Goering, Goebbels, etc. and them to their subordinates, Heydrich, Globocnik, Eichmann, etc.), to physically eradicate the Jews of Europe at the start of the Soviet Offensive in the summer of 1941. The Functionalists believe that there were no direct orders but rather it was a gradual radicalization (likely originating from the "Commissar Decree," the order to execute all Soviet political prisoners, in violation of the Geneva conventions), of the indoctrinated rank and file Nazi SS, police and Wehrmacht soldiers picking up a momentum of its own and ultimately culminating with the gas chambers.

Recent archives discovered after the fall of the Soviet Union and subsequent lifting of the Iron Curtain in 1991 containing volumes of evidence in the form of correspondence, journal entries and many other documents, indicate it was a combination of both Intentionalist and Functionalist schools of thought, and that events on the ground effected decisions at the top and vice versa.

Though the Nazis prescribed to a hierarchical, command and control system, they were very much aligned with the German Army's Prussian military roots of Auftragstaktik (mission command), which trained officers to make their own decisions on the battlefield and adapt to changing conditions as needed. Their only orders were the mission objectives, how they achieved them were up to them.

The entire German army chain of command operated this way resulting in the Wehrmacht being an extremely formidable and effective fighting force. So, in essence, the SS ideology provided a doctrinal framework, with the understanding that junior officers were allowed to act on their own initiative to obtain the desired results. Concordantly, the individual German solider was very disciplined and would relentlessly follow any tactical and strategic order given until achieved.

That coupled with the one common denominator that all loyal Nazis agreed on: the foundation of their ideology and basis for "Judenpolotik," that the Jewish race was an existential threat and must cease to exist, would inexorably lead to an intentional, physical annihilation of all Jewish men, women and children within their sphere of influence.

Once the decisions were made and wheels set in motion, this genocide was implemented and executed with brutally efficient haste. As the war lagged on, the more the Nazis needed to apply Judenpolotik to exert control over their waffling Axis allies, hence the late demise of hundreds of thousands of Hungarian, Greek, Italian and Slovakian Jews.

To the Nazis, this war was all about race and Lebensraum. The genuine belief in their very narrow worldview and race-based ideology enabled them to relentlessly pursue with absolute focus their goal of gaining totalitarian political power. Upon which success validated and further radicalized them explaining the motivation behind their conduct of the war.

As the war progressed and German casualties mounted, the more the Nazis felt the need to offset their loss of pure Aryan blood with that of the Jew and at a far greater ratio. They also believed their own rhetoric that the Jew was the ultimate manipulator and if left alive, would no doubt influence a German defeat so must be neutralized all the more quickly.

Hitler acknowledged the power of Jewish perseverance in *Mein Kampf*, writing:

"The mightiest counterpart to the Aryan is represented by the Jew. In hardly any people in the world is the instinct of self-preservation developed more strongly than in the so-called 'chosen.' Of this, the mere fact of the survival of this race may be considered the best proof. Where is the people which in the last two thousand

88

years has been exposed to so slight changes of inner disposition, character, etc., as the Jewish people? What people, finally, has gone through greater upheavals than this one and nevertheless issued from the mightiest catastrophes of mankind unchanged? What an infinitely tough will to live and preserve the species speaks from these facts!"

Armed Jewish civilian resistance to this onslaught was nearly impossible and counter-intuitive as the Germans welcomed any opportunity to justify mass killings as reprisals and ruthlessly applied a policy of collective punishment. Even for non-Jewish partisans or resistance activities, they would kill over 100 Jewish "hostages" for each German casualty. In response to Jewish revolts at the Sobibor and Treblinka death camps or at the Minsk, Vilna, and Warsaw ghettos, etc., the Germans simply executed everyone and razed the ghettos, with all their remaining inhabitants, to the ground. Any in the non-Jewish population caught assisting Jews in any way were subject to summary execution along with their immediate families and/or deportation to concentration camps.

Later in life, Bubby would often question why the world did not do more to try and stop this genocide. Though the Allies had concrete intelligence that Jews were being slaughtered in Eastern Europe, the truth of the matter is, there was not much they could have done to stop it. The targeted annihilation of the Jews began soon after the Germans invaded the Soviet Union in the summer of 1941. By that time, most of Europe was under Axis control, the United States had not yet entered the war and Great Britain was still reeling from the Battle of the Atlantic, The Battle of Britain and the North African Campaign.

In this all-out, total state of war, diplomacy was not an option. The only way to interfere would be militarily in areas where the Allies had no military presence. Infiltrating commandos/special forces deep into enemy territory to engage the Einsatzgruppen, with no actionable intelligence to when and where their small, mobile units spread out over thousands of square miles were operating, would have been a one-way suicide mission.

At the height of the Final Solution during Operation Reinhard, from the spring of 1942 to the fall of 1943 (culminating with Operation Erntefest, the mass shooting in one day of 43,000 Jews by the SS, Orpo police and their Trawniki Hiwi collaborators), there were three fixed targets to possibly bomb: the death camps of Belzec, Sobibor and Treblinka. However, at that point in the war, none were within bomber range. Even if they were reachable by a long range, high altitude bomber, and their precise locations known, the camps were small and purposely hidden by trees. With no pin point bombing capabilities at that time, they would likely not have been destroyed or even severely damaged. If so, they would have been quickly rebuilt, or new ones built at other hidden locations. Even the tracks crisscrossing Poland carrying the endless flow of Holocaust trains, though bombed from above (later in the war) and constantly sabotaged by Partisans on the ground (throughout the war), were quickly repaired.

By the end of 1943, Auschwitz was just within the maximum range of the United States Army Air Force B-17 bombers based in Foggia, Italy. An air raid on Auschwitz at that time, having to fly entirely over Axis controlled airspace there and back with no fighter escort as the long-range P-51 Mustang had not yet been introduced into service, would have come at a prohibitively high cost of aircraft and crew.

Proof of that was demonstrated by Operation Tidal Wave conducted in August earlier that year. With B-24 bombers flying from Northern Libya and Southern Italy, the USAAF attacked the oil refineries in Ploieşti, Romania. It was one of the costliest bombing missions of the war, with 53 aircraft and 660 crewmen lost in a single day. It had no significant, long term effect on the refineries' output.

As such, no more air raids were planned from that direction into Eastern Europe until later in the war. By May of 1944 however, the USAAF had the ability to bomb Auschwitz at will. In fact, on August 20, 1944, as part of their strategic bombing campaign targeting German fuel production, over 120 B-17 bombers, with an escort of 100 P-51 fighters, dropped over 1,300-500-pound bombs on the IG Farben synthetic-oil factory, which was only 5 miles from Auschwitz-Birkenau.

Auschwitz was a massive, sprawling complex comprised of many sub camps. Only one of them contained the gas chambers and crematoria, the rest housed tens of thousands of civilians and prisoners of war used for slave labor. An air raid on the camp could have resulted in massive loss of innocent life, which is why even the Jewish Agency Executive Committee meeting in Jerusalem on June 11, 1944, did not make a resolution calling for its bombing.

However, as the full scope of the atrocities at Auschwitz came to light, the policy of not diverting any military resources from the main focus of winning the war could no longer be justified. Destroying the gas chambers and crematoria at all costs became morally imperative, so in November of 1944, the decision was finally made to bomb the camp and the rail lines leading to it. By then it no longer mattered, the exterminations had stopped.

On October 7, 1944 the 12th Sonderkommando, with gunpowder smuggled to them from female prisoners working at the nearby Weichsel-Union-Metallwerke munitions factory, a couple of stolen guns, axes, knives and homemade grenades, revolted, killing and injuring a number of SS and Kapo guards and blowing up Crematorium IV. This event is depicted in the 2001 movie, "The Gray Zone." This gruesome, chillingly realistic all-star cast film is a must see to understand what happened at the Auschwitz murder factory and how it operated. Immediately after the revolt, however, the killings resumed and a new, 13th Sonderkommando pressed into service. Within a few weeks though, realizing the end to the Nazi regime was nigh, Himmler ordered the end of all gassing operations at Auschwitz.

Had the Allies and even world Jewry known that half of the over one million innocent Jewish men, women and children murdered at Auschwitz-Birkenau would be gassed and cremated from May to November 1944, they may have looked more closely at the intelligence reports and aerial surveillance photographs and decided to obliterate its murderous infrastructure from the air. This would not only have ultimately resulted in saving tens of the thousands of lives; it would have sent a powerful message to the Nazis that the Allies were well-aware of their atrocities and would not tolerate them.

Unlike earlier in the war, as mentioned above, where the Allies had no means of effectively confronting militarily the Nazi slaughter of Jews, they could have now. This would have forced the Nazis at this stage of the war to re-evaluate their genocidal policies and think twice about pursuing them. Unfortunately, only hindsight is 20/20.

It is important to note, that most of the 6 million Jews who perished in the Holocaust were killed before the Allies even landed at Normandy. The swiftness in which the Nazis executed the Final Solution was purposeful. It allowed no time for planning significant counter measures. The Nazis waged an all-out war against the Jews and the only way to stop the slaughter was to destroy the Nazis. That effort cost the lives of over 11 million Allied soldiers, the Soviet Union bearing the brunt of it with nearly 9 million.

In a way, the Nazis achieved their goal of eradicating the Jews from Europe. Before World War II there were 17 million Jews living on the continent. Now only 1.4 million, less than 10%, remain. Bubby would always express bewilderment as to how the Germans, who were so cultured and educated, could have perpetrated such an atrocity. Growing up in an affluent, educated family in Western Poland, Germany was their source of inspiration. This undoubtedly further validated her belief that if it happened there, it could happen anywhere.

Israel became a sovereign Jewish State in 1948. Many Holocaust survivor refugees soon settled there along with many North African and Middle Eastern Jews expelled by the Arabs from their home countries. More recently, Ethiopian, FSU and even North and South American and Western European Jewish immigration has added to its diversity as a homeland for all Jews.

With its current burgeoning, high-tech fueled economy and support from Jews in the Diaspora and Evangelical Christians in the United States, the State of Israel will help ensure the physical and spiritual survival of the Jewish people indefinitely.

עם ישראל חי

Am Yisroel Chai!

(The Nation of Israel Lives!)

Epilogue

Bubby passed away on March 15, 2019. She was 94 and a half years-old. She was survived by two daughters, 20 grandchildren and nearly 50 great grandchildren. She was in good health for a woman her age right up until the day she died. She passed in her sleep, comfortably in a bed with her youngest daughter Michelle by her side. She did not suffer. She had already suffered enough for a few lifetimes.

As Bubby gracefully advanced in age and into her nineties, I feared that her incredible will to live would not let her go easy, that she might linger in hospice or even on life support. Hearing of her calm and courage the day she died, I now understand where her strength came from. It was not from a fear of death, rather a love of life. She knew it was time and allowed herself to go to God and to her family that left her so long ago.

A hardworking, devoted and caring wife, mother, grandmother, great grandmother and friend, Bubby would not be defined by the persistent trauma she endured for over 5 consecutive years in the prime of her youth. It did not break or embitter her, and she passed on that love of life and optimism to her family. One of her grandchildren speaking at her funeral said it most eloquently. Bubby never saw the glass half empty or full, she simply saw the water. Whatever amount of water in the glass was good, and was all that mattered.

Bubby, like some other survivors of the Holocaust who suffered enormous loss and then had to endure the tragic loss of a child (or in Bubby's case two children and a grandchild) later in life, shared a unique perspective. They saw life as a journey, simply appreciating the time their loved ones were with them, even if they were just passing through. This outlook had to be a source of her tremendous courage and optimism.

Whenever I get despondent, all I need to do is think of Bubby for strength and realize whatever challenges I have are truly inconsequential compared to what Bubby went through.

While attending Bubby's funeral, paying my respects with scores of family, friends and those she inspired over the years, who came from near and far and sitting before her simple, traditional draped pine box casket with her grandsons and son-in-law eulogizing her from the podium above, I felt a tremendous sense of closure and peace. I realized not only were we honoring her that day, but her father and mother, her grandparents, aunts, uncles and cousins who had no funerals, have no graves and had no one to mourn for them. By surviving, living and passing on at a ripe old age in peace, Bubby not only defied the Nazis, but brought honor and closure to her family, enabling all of us to give tribute to them. Even in death, Bubby's graciousness, selflessness, respect and consideration were evident to all.

The poetic inscription on her tombstone over her eternal resting place in Jerusalem, Israel translates from Hebrew as follows:

From the ashes of the Holocaust she rose to the part; to conceal the pain encased in her heart. With her faith lived she, with all her tribulations; she renewed and built, continuity of generations. With kind eyes and caring nature; a heart full of love for every creature. Worthy was she, to live to see, her descendants follow in her footsteps and continue in her ways.

עליה השלום

Ah-layha Ha-Shalom

(May Peace be Upon Her)

זכר צדיקת לברכה

Zay-Cher Tza-Daiket L'Vracha

(May the Memory of a Righteous Woman be for a Blessing)

Made in the USA
Middletown, DE
23 November 2021